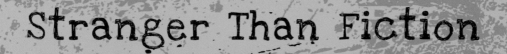

# MYSTERIOUS VANISHINGS

By Virginia Loh-Hagan

Disclaimer: This series focuses on the strangest of the strange. Have fun reading about strange people and things! But please do not try any of these antics. Be safe and smart!

## 45th Parallel Press

Published in the United States of America by Cherry Lake Publishing
Ann Arbor, Michigan
www.cherrylakepublishing.com

Reading Adviser: Marla Conn MS, Ed., Literacy specialist, Read-Ability, Inc.
Book Designer: Melinda Millward

Photo Credits: © Stone36 / Shutterstock.com, cover; © andreiuc88 / Shutterstock.com, 1; © Fer Gregory / Shutterstock.com, 5, 7; © photowrzesien / Shutterstock.com, 6; © Perkus / iStock.com, 8; © Harris & Ewing, photographer / Library of Congress, 9; © WindVector / Shutterstock.com, 10; © Robert W. Kelley / Gettyimages.com, 12; © Bettmann / Gettyimages.com, 13; © Everett Historical / Shutterstock.com, 14, 15; © Rinus Baak / Dreamstime.com, 16; © andyKRAKOVSKI / iStock.com, 17; © Jaroslaw Pawlak / Shutterstock.com, 18; © KelvinW / Shutterstock.com, 19; © Stock Montage / Gettyimages.com, 20; © Thomas Faull / iStock.com, 21; © Zack Frank / Shutterstock.com, 22; © Paul Fearn / Alamy Stock Photo, 24; © Thomas Marchhart / Shutterstock.com, 25; © f11photo / Shutterstock.com, 26; © David Clapp / Gettyimages.com, 27; © Time Life Pictures / Gettyimages.com, 28; © ASSOCIATED PRESS / Photographed by Clark [November, 26, 1971], 29; © motive56 / Shutterstock.com, 30

**45th Parallel Press** is an imprint of Cherry Lake Publishing.

Library of Congress Cataloging-in-Publication Data

Names: Loh-Hagan, Virginia, author.
Title: Mysterious vanishings / by Virginia Loh-Hagan.
Description: Ann Arbor : Cherry Lake Publishing, 2018. | Series: Stranger than fiction |
    Includes bibliographical references and index. | Audience: Grades 4 to 6.
Identifiers: LCCN 2017035393| ISBN 9781534107588 (hardcover) |
    ISBN 9781534109568 (pdf) | ISBN 9781534108578 (pbk.) |
    ISBN 9781534120556 (hosted ebook)
Subjects: LCSH: Disappearances (Parapsychology)—Juvenile literature.
Classification: LCC BF1389.D57 L64018 | DDC 001.94—dc23
LC record available at https://lccn.loc.gov/2017035393

Printed in the United States of America
Corporate Graphics

## About the Author

Dr. Virginia Loh-Hagan is an author, university professor, former classroom teacher, and curriculum designer. The only thing that vanishes in her life is the food in front of her face. She lives in San Diego with her very tall husband and very naughty dogs. To learn more about her, visit www.virginialoh.com.

# Table of Contents

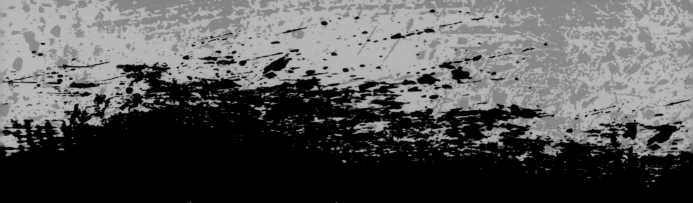

# Introduction

People lose things all the time. Things go missing. Things vanish. To vanish means to be gone. Things are here one minute. Then they're gone the next minute.

But it's one thing to lose a sock. It's another to lose people, ships, or towns! There have been some major vanishings. They can't be explained. They're unsolved mysteries. No one knows what happened.

But there are strange vanishings. And then there are really strange vanishings. They're so strange that they're hard to believe. They sound like fiction. But these stories are all true!

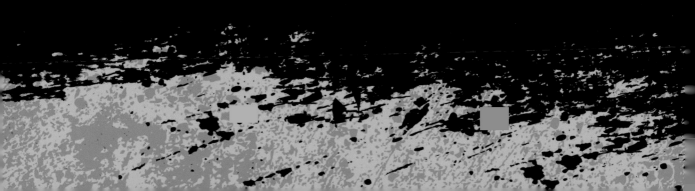

*Vanishing is another word for "disappearing."*

# chapter one

# Frederick Valentich

Frederick Valentich vanished. He was 21 years old. He flew a small plane. He flew over Australia. He used the radio. He said something was flying above him. He said, "It's not an **aircraft**." Aircraft means machines that fly.

There were strange scraping sounds. Then, contact was lost. No one heard from him again. No one saw him again. This happened on October 21, 1978. People searched for him. They looked for 4 days.

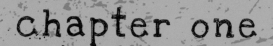

*Some people reported seeing strange things in the sky.*

Some people think aliens took him. Valentich believed in **UFOs**. UFOs are unidentified flying objects. They're thought to be alien spaceships.

# chapter two

# U.S.S. Cyclops

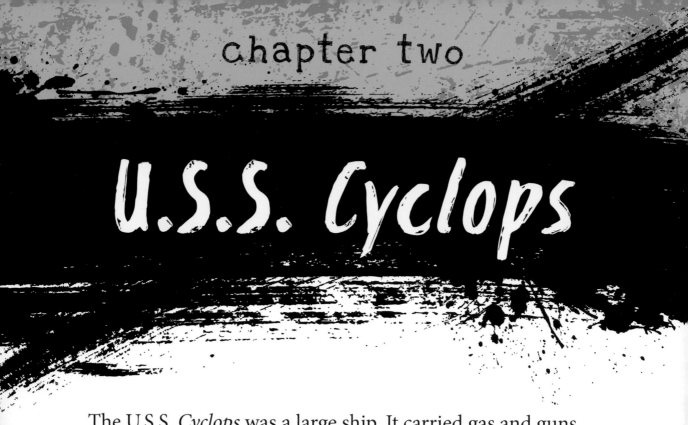

The U.S.S. *Cyclops* was a large ship. It carried gas and guns. It was last seen on March 4, 1918. There were over 300 people on the ship. The ship and the people disappeared. It was the largest loss of life outside of war in U.S. **naval** history. Naval means of the Navy.

The ship left from Brazil. It was expected in Baltimore. It never made it. The captain didn't send a help signal. No survivors were found. No **wreckage** was found. Wreckage is crash remains.

*A cyclops is a one-eyed giant from Greek myths.*

There was bad weather. The ship was having engine trouble. It was carrying a lot of stuff.

The U.S.S. *Cyclops* got lost in the Bermuda Triangle. The area is between Miami, Bermuda, and San Juan. Miami is in Florida. Bermuda is an island. San Juan is in Puerto Rico. The area is huge.

Many people, planes, and boats get lost in this area. They vanish underwater. They disappear without a trace. The Bermuda Triangle is deep. Bodies and wreckage sink. They sink too deep to be reached. There are many storms. The area has sharp ridges. It has high waves. It has strong **currents**. Currents are water flows. The area affects **compasses**. This causes confusion. Compasses are tools. They help people find places.

*Some call the Bermuda Triangle the "graveyard of the Atlantic."*

EUROPE

NORTH
ATLANTIC OCEAN

NORTH
AMERICA

Bermuda

Florida — Bermuda
triangle

AFRICA

Puerto Rico

# Explained by Science

How do magicians make things vanish? They create illusions. Illusions are tricks of the eyes. Eyes get distracted. This means they miss something. They miss small changes. David Copperfield is a magician. He made 13 people vanish. He put them inside a cage. He gave them torches. They disappeared. They reappeared at the back of the theater. How did he do this? Copperfield puts a curtain over the cage. The torchlight makes you think people are still there. But the people go down a secret door in the floor. They're rushed offstage. The audience believes what their eyes see. They can't see the trick.

# chapter three

# Jimmy Hoffa

Jimmy Hoffa was president of the Teamsters. This is the largest **labor** union in the United States. Labor means work. Hoffa broke laws. He stole money. He bribed people. He went to prison. President Nixon let him go. But Hoffa had to promise not to go back to the Teamsters. He didn't keep his promise.

He had a meeting with the **mob**. The mob is an organized group of criminals. Hoffa got to the parking lot. He waited 30 minutes. He called his wife. He hasn't been seen since. He disappeared on July 30, 1975. He disappeared around 2:45 p.m. He was 62 years old. His body was never found.

*Jimmy Hoffa was from Detroit, Michigan.*

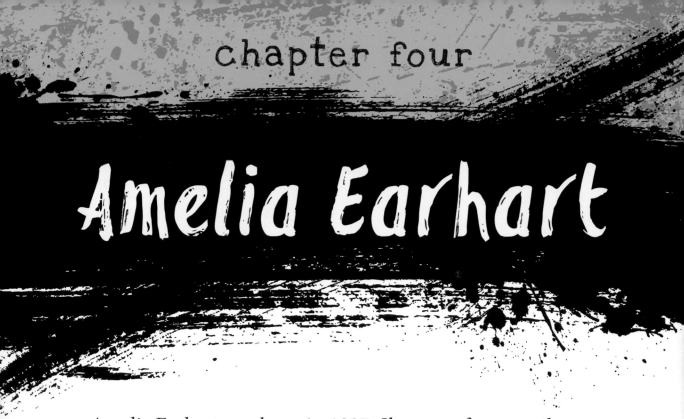

# chapter four

# Amelia Earhart

Amelia Earhart was born in 1897. She was a famous pilot. She flew across the Atlantic Ocean. She did this by herself. She was the first woman to do this. She was the first person to fly over both the Atlantic and Pacific Oceans.

In 1937, she tried to fly around the world. People think she got lost. They think she ran out of gas. She disappeared over the Pacific Ocean.

Nobody knows what happened. Some people believe she died in a plane crash. Some believe she died on a deserted island. A human skeleton was found

*Earhart was called "Lady Lindy."*

on the island. Scientists studied it. They think it's a match for Earhart. But no one knows for sure.

# chapter five

# Nome, Alaska

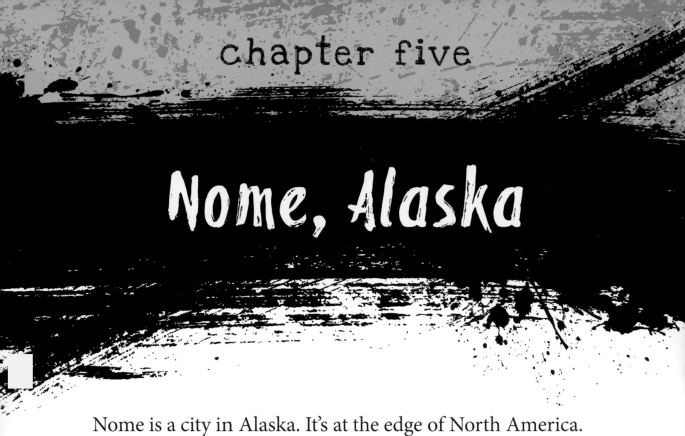

Nome is a city in Alaska. It's at the edge of North America. It's wild country. It's freezing cold. It's **remote**. Remote means far away from cities.

Twenty-four people have disappeared since 1960. Men, women, and children have disappeared. They left no trace. There were no footprints. There were no bodies. There were no clues. There are more missing persons in Nome than other places.

People worried about a **serial** killer. Serial means the same killer kills many different people. The FBI came to

16

*Over 3,000 people were reported missing in the state of Alaska.*

investigate. They found nothing. They found no one. They blamed alcohol abuse. They blamed the winter weather. People in Nome blamed aliens.

# chapter six

# The Sodder Children

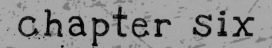

The year was 1945. It was Christmas Eve. George and Jennie Sodder had 10 children. Nine lived with them. They lived in West Virginia.

They went to bed. The phone rang. Jennie answered it. She heard a woman laughing. There were sounds on the roof. The house was on fire. George, Jennie, and four children ran out. They wanted to save the five other children. They looked for the ladder. But it was missing. They couldn't do anything. They watched the house burn down.

The other children should have died in the fire. But there were no bones. George

*The Sodders turned the land where the house was into a memorial garden to honor their lost children.*

and Jennie thought they had been kidnapped. People reported seeing them. But the five children disappeared forever.

# chapter seven

# Lost Colony

**Settlers** traveled from England. Settlers build new lives in another country. They came in 1587. They landed on Roanoke Island. This area was part of the Virginia **colony**. Colony means an area controlled by another country. Roanoke Island is about 8 miles (13 kilometers) long. It's about 2 miles (3 km) wide. It's in North Carolina.

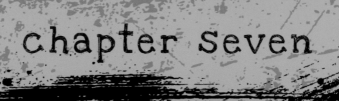

The settlers lived in Roanoke. They built houses. Life was tough. They fought against Native Americans. They ran out of food. They sent their governor, John White, back to England. They wanted him to get supplies. White went back. He couldn't leave England for a while.

*Virginia was named after the "Virgin Queen." The Virgin Queen was Queen Elizabeth.*

White returned to Roanoke on August 18, 1590. People were gone. Houses were taken down. There were no signs of struggle. There was only a fence. "Croatoan" was carved into a fence post. "Cro" was carved into a tree. Croatoan was the name of a nearby island. It was the name of a friendly Native American tribe.

White had told the settlers to carve a special cross. This would let him know they were forced to leave. He didn't see a cross.

No one knows what happened. They're called the Lost Colony. There were about 90 men. There were about 20 women. There were about 10 children.

*The settlers did not keep any records.*

# Spotlight Biography

INTERPOL is the International Police Organization. It helps find missing persons. It has a database of missing persons. Many countries share information. They send alerts of criminals. They want to catch the bad guys. Meng Hongwei was born in 1953. He went to Peking University. He studied law. He's the current president of INTERPOL. He was elected in 2016. His term will be over in 2020. He's from China. He's the first Chinese citizen to be president of INTERPOL. He has worked in criminal justice for over 40 years. Hongwei said he'd do anything he could to support "the cause of policing in the world."

# chapter eight

# Louis Le Prince

Louis Le Prince was born in 1841. He disappeared in 1890. He was from France. He invented things. He made the first movie.

He was in Dijon, France. He was visiting his brother. He was headed to New York. But he wanted to go to Paris first. He wanted to visit friends. He went on a train. He did this on September 16, 1890. The train arrived in Paris. But Le Prince didn't. His body was never found. His luggage was never found.

He was seen boarding the train. After that, no one saw him again. He was declared dead in 1897.

24

The French police, Scotland Yard, and the family searched for Le Prince. They found nothing.

# chapter nine

# Frank Morris

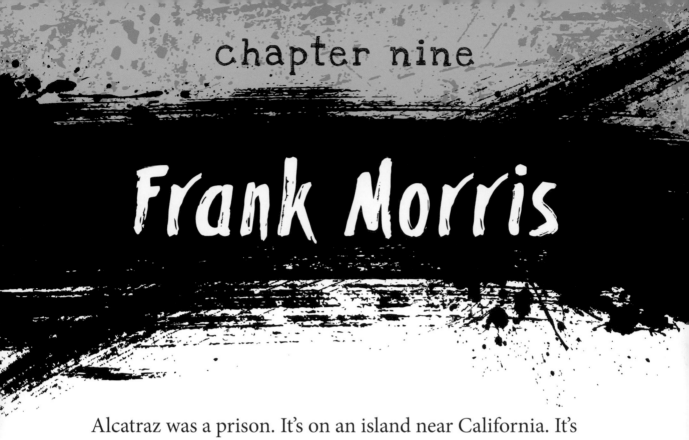

Alcatraz was a prison. It's on an island near California. It's hard to escape. But Frank Morris did it. He did it in 1962.

He planned an escape. He and two other prisoners worked at night. They made holes. They used spoons. They covered the holes with cardboard. They hid the noise by playing music. They made fake heads. They used soap and toilet paper. They put the heads in their beds. They crawled through the holes. They went to the roof. They made a boat. They used raincoats.

*Morris dug a hole out of his cell.*

They slid down a pipe. They climbed fences. They sailed away. They did this during a thick fog.

The FBI searched. No one ever found them.

# chapter ten

# D. B. Cooper

A man went to the airport. He was around 45 years old. He was around 6 feet (183 centimeters) tall. He wore a black raincoat. He wore a dark suit. He wore a white shirt. He wore a black tie. He wore dark sunglasses. He had a black bag. He bought a plane ticket. He got on Flight 305. The plane left Portland, Oregon. It was heading to Seattle, Washington. The flight was only 30 minutes long.

He sat in the back of the plane. He lit a cigarette. He ordered a drink. He gave a note to the flight attendant. He said, "Miss, you'd better look at that note. I have a bomb."

28

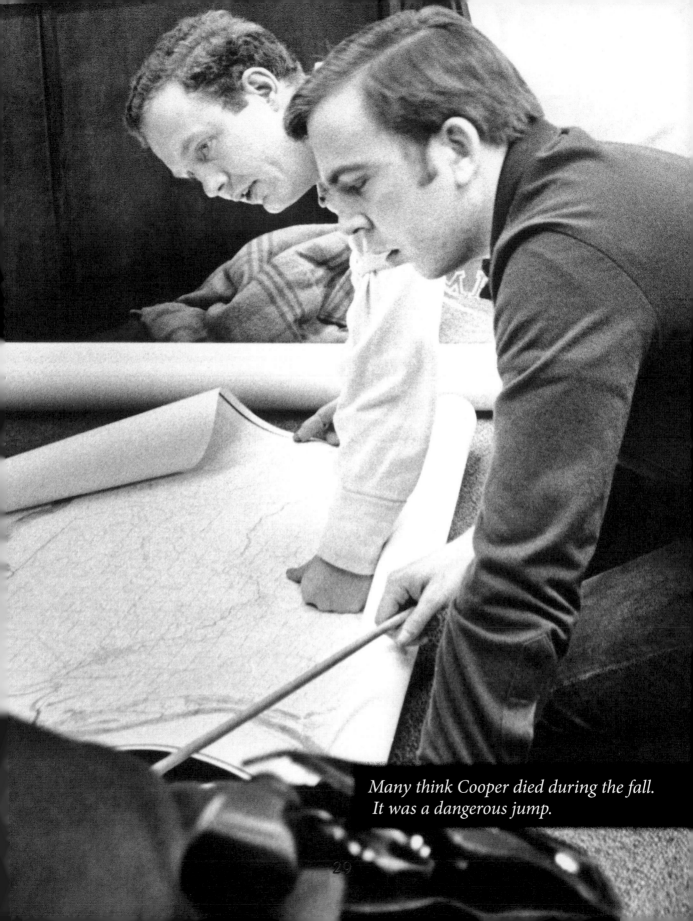

*Many think Cooper died during the fall.*
*It was a dangerous jump.*

He asked for money and **parachutes**. Parachutes slow down falls. They're like umbrellas.

The plane landed in Seattle. The airline gave him everything he wanted. The man traded passengers for the things he wanted. He told the pilot to fly to Mexico City. When they were in the air, he jumped off the plane. He used his parachute. He did this on November 24, 1971.

He used the name "Dan Cooper." But that's a fake name. He's known as D. B. Cooper. No one knows where he is. No one knows who he is. It's the only unsolved plane **hijacking**. Hijack means to take over a plane.

*The FBI searched for years. They stopped in 2016.*

# Try This!

- Play hide-and-seek. Set rules. Mark the area. Be safe.

- Vanish for a little bit. Take some "alone time." Have fun by yourself. Think about things. Challenge yourself to do something without screens.

- Visit one of the places mentioned in this book. An example is Roanoke. Take tours. Visit museums.

- Do a magic trick. Make something vanish.

- Go to your school's lost and found. Try to find the owners of the lost things.

- Create a memorial. Memorials are ways to remember people or events.

# Consider This!

**Take a Position!** If people are gone for a certain amount of time, they're declared dead. What do you think about this practice? Do you agree or disagree with it? Argue your point with reasons and evidence.

**Say What?** Research another example of a vanishing. Explain what happened. Was the mystery solved? If so, explain how.

**Think About It!** People don't like not knowing things. They want to figure out what happened. Think about some of these vanishings. What do you think happened to the people? Why do you think so?

## Learn More!

- MacLeod, Elizabeth. *Vanished: True Tales of Mysterious Disappearances*. Toronto: Annick Press, 2016.
- Matthews, Rupert. *Disappearances*. Irvine, CA: QEB Publishing, 2010.

# Glossary

**aircraft (AIR-kraft)** machines that fly, like planes and helicopters

**colony (KAH-luh-nee)** a place controlled by another country

**compasses (KUHM-puhs-iz)** navigational tools that help people find their way

**currents (KUR-uhnts)** strong flows of water

**hijacking (HYE-jak-ing)** taking over a plane or car

**labor (LAY-bur)** work

**mob (MAHB)** an organized group of criminals

**naval (NAY-vuhl)** of the navy

**parachutes (PA-ruh-shoots)** tools that help slow down a fall

**remote (rih-MOHT)** far away from cities

**serial (SEER-ee-uhl)** of a series, more than one

**settlers (SET-lurz)** people who come from another place to build a new home in a new place

**UFOs (YOO-EF-OHz)** unidentified flying objects, alien spaceships

**vanish (VAN-ish)** to be gone, to disappear

**wreckage (REK-ij)** remains at a crash site, scraps

# Index